ZIG – ZAG GIRL

Poems by
Brenna Twohy

For Oregon, my second home,
and for my mom, my first.

4

Contents

I – ZIG

II – ZAG

III – GIRL

I. ZIG

A Coworker Asks Me If I Am Sad, Still

& I tell her,

grief is not a feeling,
but a neighborhood.

this is where I come from.
everyone I love still lives there.

someday I hope to raise a family
in a place you could not mistake
for any home I've ever been in.

Brenna, she says,
        there's no such thing
                as an unhaunted house.

Conversations About Top Chef

(after Desiree Dallagiacomo)

So they take these 15 cooks, right?
& they put them together in a kitchen
& tell them to make a six course meal
out of vending machine snacks.

& then the judges say ridiculous shit, like *I wonder*
if perhaps the Bugles would have made
for a better taste contrast than the Doritos.

& then everyone says *I am not a pastry chef.*

& then everyone cooks scallops,
like all the time,
they are always cooking scallops,
& then they have to make a wedding cake
out of taco shells,

& one time, when my brother Matt was
like four years old, he went into the front yard
& he sprinkled a packet of taco seasoning
onto the soil there

& he waited for the taco shells to grow.

& my mom told him, *buddy,*
there are some things that just don't grow here,
but the next morning, she woke
at like 5 AM to go into the front yard
& push six taco shells
into the soft dirt there,
& when he saw them, he said, *I knew!*
I knew that they would grow here,
if only we let them.

& we did not have a funeral.

Just a barbecue.
Just five jumbo bags of Cheetos
& what was left of our family.

& we did not bury his body,
but if we had, I know,
nothing would have grown there.

You would not believe
the amount of salt
that most things need.

Would not believe
how hot you have to get
a pan to get a good sear on.

A week after he died, we found
my brother's Top Chef audition tape,
& it was terrible.

He's holding a blood orange
in his left hand as he cuts it
with his right, & we all watched
breathless, not knowing
where the knife would end up, &

I will never again not know
the sound of my mother breaking,
so I chew on tinfoil
& I call it a meal.

I chew on the gristle
of the last time we talked
on the phone & I do not think
I will ever be ready to swallow it.

tell me again
about the part where grief
is not my name.

I will tell you,
my parents have not kissed on the lips
since the nineties.

I will tell you,
there is so much I did not say
out of respect for the living.

I will tell you,
one of the first rules
of working in a kitchen
is you never try to catch a falling knife.

but lord, if we didn't try anyhow.
lord, if we aren't a family of good intentions

& cut off hands.

The Author Pauses
To Correct A Metaphor

Addiction is not the kitchen fire
I was warned of,

                              (It is not that gentle in its timing.
                    Doesn't torch everything you love at once
                              and leave you to rebuild it.)

or the kitchen,

                              (if you can't stand the heat
                              hold your palm to the flame
                              until you can)

or even the hunger.

                              (although, yes, it will come
                    for your empty belly with soft
                              in both its hands.)

Addiction is the feast,
the whole family gathered together
laughing, as everything they've made
is eaten away, until finally
they glance down

        to see it gone.

There's This Story Mom Tells

about these gorgeous tomato plants she was
growing in the front yard & how
I plucked each of them, green and hardened,
from the vine, piled them in my wheelbarrow,
dragged them into the kitchen, showed her
how I had helped, asked if she was proud

& she could not bring herself
to tell me what I had done.

there are these dreams I've been having
where your body is our front yard,
where our family is this barren vine,
where I am so much
wailing, unripe fruit.

you've been gone three months exactly, so
I tell strangers the story of the costume contest,

how I was little red riding hood.
how you rushed the stage,
gentle wolf.
playful snarl.
how you carried me the whole way home.

I have a wheelbarrow mouth.

I drag your name with me
everywhere I go.

Touchdown Jesus

It will take you eight minutes to drive through the entirety of La Cañada Flintridge, which accounts for you hitting all three traffic lights & for the full two minutes you will spend pulled over in the parking lot of the Lutheran church staring up at Touchdown Jesus. Touchdown Jesus is like four stories tall and carved entirely of marble. Touchdown Jesus is where we will meet you before the party, & someone will bring a bottle of whipped cream vodka & someone will bring a Costco pack of Mike's Hard & someone will give someone else a blow job like four feet away & someone will be holding my hand as we run from the cops through the too-warm night like fear is something we have any right to,

listen, this whole town is a friend you do not want
                              staying with you when they come to visit.

listen, one day all the swimming pools in all the neighborhoods will forget how to float you. listen, one time they found a colony of bees swarming in Touchdown Jesus's ear & then the church told us it had never been Jesus at all, it had been Touchdown Paul the whole time, & the entire town is like this.

they will only claim you until something in your head starts
buzzing. until something poison nests itself inside of you.

listen, I consider myself a pretty good kid but the last time I saw my brother alive we were getting high together in an alley ten minutes before family dinner

& I do not know why I am telling you this except to say
                              I have loved a man who had a swarm inside of him.

or,

                              the day he died I watched all the world's honey dissolve
                                        into a bee's mouth.

or, back home there is this hollow, buzzing body that was holy until it wasn't, which is what we do to you in this town; but one time my parents bought us a snow cone machine & we set it up on the street corner & I'm not certain, but I think it might still be there & if this whole town is a lesson on escape, I am a nest

or a hive

or a swarm
bumping up against the edges of an eardrum

and calling it the entire world.

Draco Malfoy
Looks Into The Mirror of Erised

& the portraits fade from his mother's walls.
Narcissa sips Firewhiskey with a different man,
his hair dark and simple.

Maybe he has a mole on his jawline.
Maybe he has an accent only when he's been drinking.
Maybe they have a beautiful daughter
whose forearm bears nothing
but her own skin.

There is no kind way to tell this story,
so I may as well tell it true,
you would not wish yourself upon anyone.

& how else to explain grief
but as this mirror?

This impossible joy
that will not let you hold it.

This mirror that slips rocks
into your pocket & reminds you

everyone you love
has a river's mouth.

February

& I don't understand how people can say the word "heaven" like it isn't a swear word. like it doesn't make my mama gasp, press her whole hand to her mouth, & wonder who taught you to say that shit in polite company. because really, when you say *"heaven,"* it's just a shined-up way of saying *"not here,"* so either way, we're left holding not-enough hands and trying to remember how to set a smaller table. two weeks ago, I got a bloody nose as the plane took off, & no one seemed to notice, so I just shoved damp red napkins into all my pockets, and it has been like this ever since. strangers smile at me on the street, & I want to press my palms right into their faces– *can't you see?*

Can't you see I'm bleeding on everything?

Mondegreen

In 1997,
three days before my mother's birthday,
Chumbawamba releases the iconic classic
Tubthumping,

& everyone I know
spends the next ten years trying to unremember it,
but despite our best efforts,
any time we walk into a Red Robin or a Spencer's Gifts,
we will *all* sing along loudly,

"I get knocked down, but
I get up again, and
you're never gonna keep me down,"

with the notable exception of my brother,
who will sing
just as loudly,

"I get knocked down, but
I can opera sing, and
I'm never gonna lose my voice."

It's called a mondegreen,
a misheard lyric,

like how the Ramones will sing,
"I wanna be sedated,"
& my mom will nod in agreement as she sings,
"I want a piece of bacon."

It's the way our brains fill in gaps,
make sense of things we didn't
or couldn't

hear,
the way my mom said,
"he's gone,"

& I asked her where,

how I could not make sense of it,
even though I had played this song for a decade,

lip-syncing the chorus every time
my phone rang in the middle of the night,
& still, I did not recognize it when it played.

My brother had a compass
with each of our names
tattooed on his chest,
and on the plane my mom said,
"I want to have that, you know."

& of course she meant the compass.

but I thought she meant his skin.

A person who used to be me
wrote a poem that same morning,
& now I do not understand the words,

or the conversations
of anyone who did not know him,

never played him in dominos
or listened for the sound of his breathing
across a hallway and two closed doors;

Spring has come so early
I must be mishearing it;

We clean out his trailer &
there is nothing there to make sense of,

an unopened bag of Swedish Fish,

and the space where they found his body.

The last thing he sent his friend Alex
was a quote from a poem I wrote years ago
about how difficult it was to love him.

I want to tell him,

this whole time--
I've been shouting the wrong words.

but I'm learning,
and I promise
I'm never gonna lose my voice.

Spoiler Alert

I.

I was snooping in mom's jewelry box
when I found the teeth,
jumbled up in a folded envelope
that rattled like a pack of Chiclets when
I shook it.

II.

When my brother came home
with his first tattoo,
mom laid the spoon carefully
across the top of the simmering pot,
then opened the leftmost drawer
& pulled out the cheese grater,
only half-joking about scraping it
off his skin.

(Spoiler alert: The brother in this story is dead now).

III.

I opened the envelope
just enough to peek inside.

Are these mine?
All of yours, she said.

All my babies' baby teeth.

IV.

When we would play hide & seek,

22

I went for the same spot each time.

There was this tiny door
in the middle of my wall that
led to a laundry hamper &
a door on the other side
leading to mom & dad's room.

I would pile dirty clothes
onto myself & hide
there, an unwashed thing.

(Spoiler alert: The me in this story is dead now.)

V.

He sent me a text ten days before he died
& I did not respond to it.

& I have not forgiven this.

VI.

I asked why I was the only one
in the family with green eyes.

Those are your baby eyes,
my brothers said. *One day they'll
fall out and your grown-up eyes
will come in.*

VII.

My first Christmas back from college,
he took all of the Xanax from my purse.

& I have not forgiven this.

VIII.

Once, when I was four or five, mom
found me asleep in the hamper
hours later, waiting
to be found.

IX.

I used to wiggle my teeth until they bled,

then cry about the bleeding. I thought I

would have more time

to tell these stories. Even

the ones that split my gums. Even when

they came in crooked & eventually

I yanked them out.

I don't know
what to do with these sharp
& mouthless memories,

this envelope of loose teeth.

II. ZAG

Swallowtail

The medical history form reads, "Has someone physically, sexually, or emotionally abused you?" with a box for yes and a box for no.

☐   I am mostly fine

☐   I am mostly fine but

☐   One Thanksgiving his mom told me this story about how as a child he found a butterfly in the yard with half a wing missing. He cupped it in his hands, brought it inside, and held it covered against his stomach for fear it would fly away. They called the animal hospital on the landline and were instructed to carefully clip the healthy wing to match the broken one.

☐   A cage of gentle
hands is still a cage,
and I know this now.

☐   I would have climbed in the jar if he'd asked me.
I would have torn the good wing off myself.

Hey, Jeff Probst!
I Wanna Be On Your Show.

I wanna lay in hammocks
and say shit like,
I'm not here to make friends,
because when I say that
in my everyday life
people look at me like
I am an unpleasant person
to be around.

Hey, Jeff Probst!
I like the parts where you have auctions
because that is like real-life eBay
or perhaps
just like a regular auction,
I don't really know,
I don't get out a whole lot.

Hey, Jeff Probst!
I do not like the part
where you make them eat things
like alive snakes
let's please not do that on our season.

Jeff,
two years ago,
a woman talked about her abuse
around your campfire.
Then, after the commercial,
a man said he understood why
her father had beaten her,

said he would have done it too,

& you poured it into my living room,
as easy as ratings.

To be an abuse survivor
is to be the worst kind of thirsty;
surrounded by water that
will kill you if you drink it,
as everyone on the shoreline says,

just look
at all that
gorgeous ocean.

Jeff,
when I left him,
he rented a U-Haul &
he moved me into my new house.

We fell asleep
on a twin mattress
on the concrete floor,

which is the softest name I have for drowning.

You have to understand,
after you realize it's a mirage,
it is sometimes simpler to
just keep calling it an island.
Calling him a good man.
Even as the water fills your lungs.
Even as you watch your body sinking.

Jeff,
what do you know about saving yourself?
& all its wretched gasping?

What do you call womanhood
if not endurance? The ways we
withstand that which we did not
believe withstandable, and then
put our own holy hands to work.

Call me Survivor.
It is the ugliest triumph I own,
but it is mine.
It is mine.

In My Dream Last Night
My Abuser Was Watching Star Wars
With My New Boyfriend

who only knows
a few parts of the story.

(I didn't want that man's name
back in my bed.)

just told him,
picture yourself in a theater
with your eyes closed,
your own palms pressed tightly to your ears.

on the drive home,
your abuser will describe each scene frame-for-frame,
talk about the previews, which one
the two of you should not-see together next,

& months later,
when he claims it is your favorite movie,
you will nod and know it is
not worth arguing over.

("are you trying
to tell me
you
weren't
even
there?")

you'll tell yourself it's true.

tell yourself
it's the best movie
you've ever seen.

Shell Game

The magician places three shells on a table, then hides a ball under one of the shells. The magician moves the shells around, then asks you which one has the ball underneath.

I.

We got the turtle one Christmas
in the mid-nineties, when we all
got jammies Christmas Eve &
Santa still brought the tree down the chimney.

He had dark orange patterns on his shell
and a tiny black Sharpie dot
on his underside that I marked there
one afternoon, a selfish secret.

We built him a box in the backyard;
fed him carrots & took him out
to crawl up and down our arms. We
named him Hector, after the man
who gave him to us, my Nana's
boyfriend, a man with a strong laugh
and the same three jokes.

I don't know how long Hector
(the turtle) was gone, the first time,
before we noticed the empty box.
He didn't leave a note.

II.

The magician is using more than one ball.

III.

It wasn't until a decade later
I found out from my Nana what
Hector (the man) had done to her.

The way their home
became a box she didn't know
if she could climb out of.

IV.

You will never guess the correct shell.
This is the way the game is designed.

V.

I found Hector (the turtle)
like two years later, knew him
from the dot on the bottom
of his shell, held open my hands
& he crawled into them like
he'd never been gone.

The first time I left my partner,
I came back within the week.

& I don't like to talk about this part.

The way I told my friends,
it's going to be better
as I fit myself back inside my shell.

I know a thing or two
about legacy.

VI.

The magician shows you there's nothing
under the shell you pointed to,

then lifts it again to reveal the ball beneath,
transported.

VII.

& what am I now
if not an empty shell? I thought

as my phone started to ring.

On the other end, my favorite voice
& the same three apologies.

This is how we learn staying.

VIII.

This is the way the game is designed.

IX.

When he finally stopped
singing *come home*,
I was not relieved.

There is more than one way
a heart can break.

X.

I'm trying to be better
about forgiveness. & this, too,
is a slow and painful unpacking,

the shedding of so many
unneeded shells.

When He Tells The Story

he cracks a joke about
dodging a bullet.

When I tell the story,
there is still a bullet, finally
done kissing the gun on his mouth.

III. GIRL

Today I Am Tired Of Being A Woman

you know that poem
about the icebox and the plums?

i've always thought
it would be nice
to be an icebox.

instead of a wanted thing.
instead of a grabbing hand.

i have practice in the art
of being cold on purpose.

how else
to keep the inside from spoiling?
to keep the rot from creeping in?

Colfax

Walking home[1]
I play the voicemail again[2],
and again[3]
and then I do the dishes
and get into bed.[4]

---

[1] past the bar where I turned twenty two,
   the bar where we fought about the right way
   to tie a cherry stem with your tongue
   which is, of course,
   to leave it in the glass

[2] & I like to think I'm three years smarter,
   but I'm just three years used
   to the way you wink
   when you say anyone's name

[3] look, I wouldn't be lying
   if I said you know me the best of anyone,
   but that truth
   is my least favorite thing about me

[4] & you are not there,
   the kindest thing
   you have ever done.

My Therapist Asks Me
To Describe You

so I tell her about the house
on Amherst, the for sale sign,
the stupid purple blinds;

tell her about that Papa Murphy's
that used to be a Blockbuster,
the way you tried to rent movies there
for like three years after
because you knew it made me laugh;

say,
have you ever come home to find the doors locked,
your key in a coat pocket on the bedroom floor,
had to break your own window with a flowerpot?

I say,
if those years were a place
they would have to be the yellow line,
an overcrowded train
hurtling in your direction;

I say,
there was not room enough
in my heart for the both of us.

Tonight
I will fall asleep next to a man I love,

which is the only thing
you and he have in common.

& what a blessing
this silly, boring love is.

the way I do not lose myself in him.
the way I am not lost at all.

the peaches shrivel on the counter,

refusing to make themselves into jam.

& what an insolent woman I have become,
knowing exactly how sweet I am
on a hungry man's tongue, and still --

call it rotting if you need to.
I'll stay till all my skin gives out.

ugly
        & uncontained.

YNAB

My budgeting software tells me I have $16 left for alcohol for the month of April & my budgeting software reminds me that this means I've already spent over half my monthly allotment & it's only been two days & my budgeting software is disappointed in me.

My budgeting software says I have $0 left for "household goods" which means I cannot buy sponges & have to wash dishes with my bath towels until May or maybe June depending on whether or not my budgeting software thinks I have learned my lesson.

I paid my rent on time! I tell my budgeting software, & my budgeting software drops the "money to pay rent" balance down to $0, then says nothing, because my budgeting software is a budgeting software and has no incentive to be proud of me.

My budgeting software noticed that I spent $20 on orange juice & categorized it as "medical expenses" & my budgeting software reminds me that I still haven't gone to a doctor, but instead bought a family pack of gummy vitamins & my budgeting software does not think this is a long-term solution.

My budgeting software thinks maybe one day I would like to see the Atlantic Ocean. Thinks everything feels better after a home-cooked meal from my mother's handwritten recipe, and thinks I deserve it every time. Thinks I do not mean it when I say *anxiety and I have gone to battle and it has won.*

My budgeting software knows exactly what I pray to.
    & what a god tomorrow is.
        & what else but a miracle, the way we go on.

The First Sarah Connor

My partner leaves me
and Buzzfeed encourages me
to try pilates.

To buy a new set of sheets.

I tell my friends loudly, *I will not wallow*
as I purchase $40 of cereal marshmallows from the internet
in a transaction I will later come to regret
both for the resulting identity theft
but also because I really wanted those cereal marshmallows
and don't know if I can handle another disappointment.

Buzzfeed says,
go to a new bar and flirt with a stranger.

I get stoned with my mother's friends
and watch the classic 1984 breakup film
The Terminator,
not-not-crying as Arnold takes the screen,
all smoke and metal, and

what more could you ask for than this?

to be huge and loud and indestructible?

listen, I know exactly how too-much I am,
I have lived in this machine my whole life,

this is not the first time love has left me
scratching at my skin,
praying to withstand just one more burning,

Buzzfeed believes I would benefit from a meal kit service.

I pause the movie to curate a plate of Oreos,
Waffles & Syrup on a bed of Double Stuf,
then carefully place the Fireworks Oreos
in the garbage where they belong,
because they are just second-rate Pop Rocks
and I deserve better than that shit.

Onscreen, Arnold tosses a guy from a phone booth,
flips through the listings until he finds *her*,

and as he pulls up to the driveway,
I am the only one holding my breath.

Arnold knocks on the door and it opens,
he says Sarah Connor?
and she says,
yes,
(her only line in the movie)
and then he shoots her like twenty-two times,
and moves on to the next Sarah Connor in the phone book.

Six months ago,
my friend Megan asked me, *do*
you think you would marry him?
and I laughed into the phone, said
that would be a disaster,

meant,
that would be a disaster, but
I'd do it in a heartbeat if he asked,

meant,

of course, I'm not the one he's looking for
but goddamn
if it didn't sound like it
when he said my name.

On Kissing The Next Boy

I had forgotten the way
a man's mouth can
be only his mouth

& not an overdue apology

or a staircase
between two unmoving doors

can you taste him I do not ask

the way
he heated water on the stovetop
when my bath ran cold

the way I loved him
exactly the wrong amount

just enough to wreck me
but not enough to stay

the way I kissed him
for the last time
like the outbreath on a sucker punch

like an undone whistle

An Honest Apology to His Wife, Ending In My Ugliest Lie

There's this technique in magic called the double lift. You tell your spectator that you're going to turn over the top card, then you turn over a card and tell them it's the top one but really you've turned over two cards at once so the card that you're showing them, the card that you're both calling "the top card" is really the second one down. When he said, *Read me a poem. I want to see what your mouth looks like with all that art inside of it*, I almost asked him to marry me that night. Didn't see the way he hid your name. Let him call me *darling* and didn't look at it too carefully. Wouldn't want to spoil the trick. Why insist on ruining magic. I am not a strong swimmer. Twice now, I have had to scream for help from the water. Both times, I thought I was fine until I wasn't. When you're drowning, a lot of things look like a raft. Even a man with a wedding ring. Even as he's pouring water down your gasping throat & calling it wine. Even a cheap miracle looks like a lantern in the winter. I'm sorry, which does nothing. He didn't tell me about you.

I didn't know.

& Her Response

You

second

mouth

the

way   you

insist on ruining

a raft.
a wedding ring. Even as
your
gasping throat
looks like
winter.
do   not   tell
me   you

didn't know.

Zig-Zag Girl

Instructions to the magician:

Position the device halfway between the audience and the curtain. Select your assistant with precision. Ensure she is accustomed to fitting herself in small spaces. Insert the bottom blade first (to build suspense). Then the neck. Slide her middle out, gently. Show the device from all angles. Let the audience marvel at the thing that you have done.

Instructions to the assistant:

the night before, dress only
in your grandmother's earrings.
lotion your un-wounded stomach.
boil water; fill the tub. practice
easing your legs in until you can do it
without flinching, a graceful sight.
The Simmering Girl.

as the first blade goes in,
recite state capitals. do not
let your face reveal the secret,
the unfortunate marrow of you.
Helena, Lansing, Des Moines.
this is not the first time you've
been pulled apart by the middle.
Dover, Richmond, Santa Fe.

there is no noticeable difference
between being whole and
being held together.
let the crowd clap, call you
a broken thing rebuilt.
& indeed, what magic --
the way you keep your blood
from touching anybody's hands.

This Time I Hope To Love Him Kindly, & From Far Away

The postcard has no signature,
says only "HOME SOON,"
in the blocky letters of that one summer
he reached for my laugh
like the last middle piece of a jigsaw
he was determined to finish before nightfall.

& I do not want to fall in love with him,
not this time,
not again.

I print out that picture of him mid-sneeze
& hang it above my dresser.

Just look at his messy.
His exploding, dangerous mouth.

I love myself best when I am the only one doing it.

I nail the mailbox shut.
I put kerosene in all the lamps.

I Am Not Clinically Crazy Anymore

according to the paperwork
& the new prescription.

but
there's this spot on the sidewalk
along the way to work
where for almost three months
there was this dead rat
& every time I passed it I thought,

someone should do something
about this dead rat

or,

I should do something
about this dead rat

then held my breath
& kept walking.

& almost a year later,
every time I pass it
I think

that's the spot
where the dead rat
used to be.

where no one did anything
for so long.

I have not almost-killed-myself
in two years and three months,

but

I look at old poems and think,

someone should do something
about this bleeding body.

my mouth,
the space
where a dead thing used to live,

even now.

when the crazy came back

she didn't throw out all the dinners,
spill the wine down my boring throat.

she didn't look anything like the last time.
didn't pound the door in.

she knows this house too well by now,
knows I'll let her in by nightfall.

I could set my watch by the knocking.
I plant dahlias in spring

& come October panic blooms
in every window box, the crazy gathers it up.

washes a vase by hand.
she has learned to be a gentle houseguest.

to seal the windows up for winter.
we could almost forgive last autumn.

the pills from my dead grandmother's purse,
that man & his wedding ring,

the way the crazy called herself my name
& I almost let her keep it.

this body knows fear like a front porch
knows welcome, it is always coming home.

& you cannot pull the crazy out of me
the way you cannot put a flower back to bed,

but this body knows withstand. knows
what the morning looks like when she says *stay*.

the crazy
is a quitter.

you have a perfect
attendance record for this life.

& I will stay.
& I will stay.

Author's Note

I am endlessly grateful to each person who has shown up for me over the last year and a half. Thank you for letting me be a mess when I needed to, and helping me carry the grief when it was too heavy to carry alone, which was every day. Megan, Gabe, Melanie, Erin, Mia, Petra, Zak, Clementine, Cam, Doc, Clayton, Amelia, Catie, Brigitte, and Mose– I could not have made it through without you.

Alban Fischer, thank you for designing my Dream Cover, it is exactly perfect.

To my family – everything good in my life is because of you.

About the Author

Brenna Twohy is a poet and performer currently living in Ann Arbor, Michigan. She is a three-time National Poetry Slam competitor and a two-time Portland City Slam Champion. Her favorite sentence is, "Do you want to see a magic trick?" This is her second collection.

Printed in Great Britain
by Amazon